Finding Your Wings to Fly

PAUL DENGLER

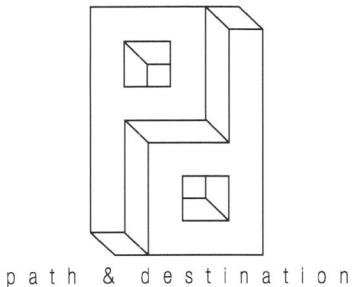

path & destination

Finding Your Wings to Fly

Copyright © 2020 by Paul Dengler

Cover Design: Christine Dupre, Vidal Design Services
Back Cover Illustration by Greg Williams of *The Villages Daily Sun*
Published by: Path & Destination Media

ISBN: 978-0-578-71871-2
Printed in the United States of America

Surely he will save you from the fowler's snare and from the deadly pestilence.

He will cover you with his feathers, and under his wings you will find refuge; his faithfulness will be your shield and rampart.

Psalm 91:3-4, NIV

What is art? Art can mean so many different things to different people at different times, but maybe art is mostly about finding the beauty in some aspect of creation and then putting a frame around that beauty so that others can experience it in the very same way that we experienced it, saw it, heard it, felt it or understood it. Maybe one of the functions of art is about finding the fingerprints of the Creator in some little corner of creation and then pointing those fingerprints out to others, putting a frame around them, and asking people to stop and take a look. In that respect, art can be a way for us to sense the invisible hand of the Creator, and then have that hand pull us up to a higher vantage point, allowing us to see things from a higher ground, with greater clarity and insight. Art lifts our spirits as it lifts our focus.

Writing is an art form, too, and this book of mine is a collection of things that I was thinking, hearing, experiencing and writing over a 7 year period, in my own little corner of the Cosmos (Nashville, Tennessee). It's a collection of my observations about myself, about my life and about my world (and about God...or at least what I think I know about God). It's a book about seeing God's fingerprints on my own life, and it's a book about my attempts to reach toward that invisible hand of God, asking God to grab hold of me and pull me to higher ground. We each have our struggles in life with those things that seem to be holding us back and keeping us down. Art has the ability to lift our spirits as it lifts our focus. Art can be a little window into Heaven, and it can, also, help bring a little bit of Heaven to Earth. We all want to rise above the things that are holding us down. Art can help us find our wings to fly. That's what this book is about: my own journey (and my journaling) toward finding my wings to fly.

on
EARTH
as it is
in
Heaven

(art is finding the beauty in Creation)

Seconds, minutes, hours and days...

days, weeks, months and years...

Seasons pass and decades flash.

A whole lifetime disappears.

Looking back you wish you had...

a new life to begin.

Truth is you do. You can start anew...

in this moment that you're in.

Sometimes you need to have a breakdown before you can have a breakthrough.

You may think the walls falling down around you is a bad thing, but maybe those walls are not protecting you like you thought anyway. Maybe they are just keeping you trapped in a stuck situation. Your breakdown might actually be the very breakthrough you've been looking for. Once those walls have fallen, you may finally be able to see that there are wide open vistas of possibility surrounding you...wide open spaces and new horizons you never saw before.

Expanding past old boundaries that no longer contain you. Growing through old contours that no longer define you. There is pain in growing through the old you into the new you.
The cracking shell of the baby bird entering a new world...or the caterpillar that went into the cocoon and emerged from the chrysalis transformed. You may think this is the end. You may feel like you're dying, but this is not your tomb...this is just your changing room.

Soon you will find your wings to fly.

If you don't know your own power, you'll always be waiting for others to provide what you already have inside. Self-doubt can spiral you into paralysis. Trust your intuitions. God made you just the way you are for a reason.

Trust that. Believe it. Walk confidently in the gifts God's given you. You were made unique for a reason. Everything will begin to unfold just as it should...as you start walking down the path of your purpose.

Real flesh and blood people can make mistakes, can offend each other, can hurt one another, and can have broken relationships as a result. Those things can really happen, and they do. Look around, you don't have to look very far to see it. But something else is also real... and it's actually really possible:

Saying you're sorry is real.

Asking for forgiveness is real.

Forgiving that other person is real, too.

Fixing and restoring your broken relationship can happen, and if you need to do that with someone in your life, you can make that real today. Don't go another day without it.

Who wants to fail? No one does, but each failure is really just a stepping stone toward your success. It's just part of the process. Don't see your failures as obstacles that make you retreat. Learn from them. They are stepping stones. Press on. Don't quit. Keep walking. You're going to get there.

Opposites don't have to live in opposition. Extreme differences don't have to divide, but can actually be the basis of cooperation and unity. Which are better: your hands or your feet? Totally depends on whether you're walking or holding something. Hands and feet might be different, but they are each a part of the same body, and each of them serve the greater good of that body. Friendship is better than fighting. We can live in peace or in pieces.

That's our choice.

A change of heart will change your life. Your heart is the central issue. Favor and blessings are just waiting to overflow into your life, but that overflow comes from your heart. From the overflow of the heart, the mouth speaks. What you think, say and do all comes from your heart. It's the source of the springs of your life. Everything wells up from there. It's not about a job change, a change of address, or some change of status. The real issue is your heart. Change your heart and watch your whole life change...just like that. It's the heart of the matter.

Do today...

what you won't regret tomorrow.

Your path from A to B probably won't be a perfectly straight vertical line. The trajectory to your goal may take you all over the map, and might look like a jumbled scribble of chaos. Sometimes going forward may even involve going in reverse. Don't get discouraged. Don't give up. Your difficult circumstances are not obstacles meant to deter you. They are meant to change you, to purify you, to refine you, and to prepare you. When you get where you're headed, your head and heart will be ready. Looking back, you'll understand that God had you go that way for a reason.

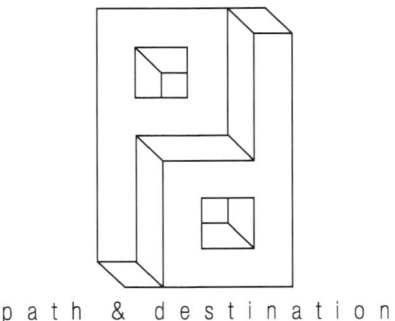

path & destination

Purify your heart and renew your mind. Live in peace, harmony and love. Be in oneness with God and the people around you, and remain in that headspace and heart-space. If something shakes you and derails you, get back on track right away. Leave the old you and your past behind. It no longer defines you.
Keep heading in the right direction.
Everything you really want is on that trajectory.
God is the path, the journey, and the destination.
Keep going.
God will get you there.

Sometimes the answer is
to just keep going.
Don't stop to act or react.
Don't orchestrate an outcome.
Just keep walking where
God is leading. Keep hoping,
trusting and believing.
The solution is up ahead.

Love gives us
wings to fly.

There's the ideal and then there's the real. You can be so attached to your high ideals that you end up missing out on what is real. Impossible standards of how your family "should" be, and how the people around you "should" be...those impossible standards can make you miss out on the good of how things actually are. If people never please you and satisfy your expectations, maybe the issue isn't with them. Maybe the problem is with your expectations. If you continually raise the bar just beyond everyone's reach, at some point, people will stop reaching. There is a balance between the pursuit of excellence and being content.

Love and accept people as
they are and where they are.
Give people love, and they
will become lovable.
Give people trust, and they
will become trustworthy.
Give people friendship,
and they will learn how to
become friends.

Pet peeves are wild creatures
that can't be tamed.
Put them out of your house before
they devour you.
Who wants to have cherished
annoyances and grievances anyway?
Give them up,
and let them go.
You're better off without them.

Look for the good in everyone, not the bad. Bring out their best, not their worst. Believe, hope, trust, encourage, and elevate. The right word at the right time can change somebody's whole life. Little acts of kindness can change the world.

GROW,

GIVE

&

CREATE.

Down, but never giving up.
Flawed, but forever leaning
in the direction of perfection.
Missing it, but always aiming higher.
Failing forward. Falling upward.
Never letting your mistakes take you out.
Making mistakes, but then making
revisions. Always not quite getting it,
but never ever quitting.
The joy is in the journey.
The path is the destination.
You're not there, but you're getting there.
Keep going.

Have you heard? Random acts of love, kindness and affection are breaking out all over. People everywhere are actually nurturing, growing and creating. Some people (whose desire it is to stir-up dissent and unrest) are troubled by these events. They want people divided, polarized and fighting. Maybe those people need a hug. Love is the catalyst, and the reaction is powerful. Show it, give it, and share it today. We all need love.

Giving is a river.

It empties to the sea.

The sea sends clouds with rain.

It makes the river be.

So, give to overflowing,

without a thought or care.

More rain will come your way.

Endless blessings fill the air.

Trusting in the left wing

and

trusting in the right wing...

of the Dove of Peace.

Trusting in the right wing

and

trusting in the left wing...

of the Dove of Peace.

Your physical enemy is not your real enemy. There are unseen forces that stir up trouble and conflict, and then watch us all destroy one another. Don't be a puppet. Cut those strings. Forgive and love your enemy. Do good to people who are not being good to you. Turn the other cheek. Quit making plans for retaliation and revenge. Be a peacemaker instead. The truth is that goodness will defeat evil. Hatred may be contagious, but love is the cure.

Hate may be contagious, but love is the cure.

Beautiful diversity

that's wonderfully interconnected

in unity,

in peace,

in harmony,

and in love.

Love is what holds us together.

There is no "us" without it.

If you want a
peaceful world,
then be peaceful.

If you want a
world that's kind,
then be kind.

Half of me and half of you:

A child is that one from two.

One plus one equals three:

The math of love and family.

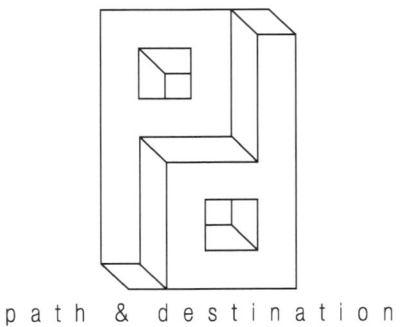

path & destination

What is really valuable?
You are the one who has value. God's
imprint on you is what gives you
value. Your unique talents, your skills,
your abilities, your personality, they
are what make you priceless. You
have so much to give.

Love is the path,

the journey,

and the destination.

The ends don't justify the means. Every step along the way is consistent with your destination.

What you're doing is where you're headed.

Holding a grudge is a
disease that will steal,
kill and destroy.

Do you want to start
living again?

Start forgiving again.

Maybe life is like music. There may be many notes, but they all fit together as part of a greater melody. Dissonance happens, but harmony is the rule. Tension builds, but resolution wins in the end. Notes leave and then return...back to the beginning, back to the source, back to the tonic. We each are parts of that song. Everything is going to fit together in time.

In time, it's all going to fit together.

Keep listening.

Keep playing.

Keep going.

The truth is we are conduits. Everything we have to give was first given to us. Being empty of yourself will allow more to flow through you. Humility is freeing and expansive. Humility sees and is connected to the bigger picture, but self-seeking only ever finds itself, and how limited is that? There's an abundance that's ready and waiting to flow through you. If you want it all just for yourself, you will only be a blockage to the flow. Get out of the way, and more will flow through you.

We receive all we're willing to give.

Let it go, and watch it flow.

Doing what you love is what others love about you. The joy of being in the zone of your calling is both a joy you feel and a joy you give. You can only be what you are. Trying to be what you're not is like an eagle trying to be a dolphin. An eagle may be able to swim for a bit, but it was really designed to fly. If God gave you wings, then you were meant to use them.

Your sky is waiting.

By the way, dolphins are unique and wonderful, too. If that's you, your ocean of possibilities awaits you.

What we dwell on becomes our dwelling.
We end up living out and living in the very
destination we envisioned in our heads.
Your life is an overflow of all you allowed in
your head and heart. Be careful about what you
let enter your eyes and ears. It becomes the
blueprint for the life you create.

What is your goal? What is your dream?

What you think you will do,
that is what you end up doing.

What you think...you will do.

It's vampiric. Negativity has a way of biting you and turning you into one of its own, but being bitten doesn't determine your destiny. That's a choice you make. Don't become bitter.

Forgive.

Love.

Do good.

Don't get bitter. Get better.

Make no decisions in those moments when you have no faith in the future. When your faith runs out, wait it out.

Things will be looking different tomorrow.

It's always been true that what you need shows up when you need it. Things materialize in uncanny and unexpected ways. Last minute miracles can and do happen, and those eleventh hour interventions from above are faith builders. Don't freak out. You may be down for the count, but it's not over yet.

Keep looking up.

Trust.

Believe.

There's no other concept quite as oppressive as the idea of "normal" or "average." Truth is we all have received a portion of the same divine spark from our Creator. Throw your comparison and envy away. We each are vessels with a unique impression. God's given each of us worth. There's treasure in each of us. We've all been created for a purpose, a unique role, a one of a kind niche that is truly like no other.
Discover your own wonderfulness.
It's there.
Believe it, and then be it.

Comparison leads to endless
emptiness and unhappiness,
but contentment is a place
of peace and joy.

An outward change is
not where it begins.
The world needs a
revolution of the heart...
one heart at a time.
Real transformation
ripples out from there.

Well said words are just that: they are coming from a deep well of experience and truth. When you hear them, you recognize them. Your own deep well of experience is tapped, too, and those deep truths that you never knew that you knew are suddenly gushing out into full view. When someone has really nailed it, what they've done is tapped into the well of truth.

We're not supposed to let the sun go down on our anger (let alone days, months and years). If you have issues with someone, you need to resolve that today. Apologize, forgive, do whatever it takes to turn the situation around. You may not have another opportunity. Own up to your part in the conflict, and release that other person from theirs. The result will be a clean slate, a clean heart, a new day, and a fresh new start for everyone involved. Get out from under the invisible burden that's weighing you down. Let it go. Forgive.

The love of power is what's wrong with the world.

What it needs is the power of love.

Some people will mock you because they believe they're masters at chess when you still haven't even learned to play checkers yet, but the main thing to remember is this: it's all just a game, and you don't even have to play it. You are the one who chooses to be a part of their head games (or not). Walk away and be free.

We all have our unique challenges and issues. Yours aren't mine and mine aren't yours, but we all have our struggles, and those struggles make us rely on God's strength to get us through. The unique mess in your own life will one day become your unique message, and your personal tests will one day become your testimony. One day, you're going to be able to tell everyone what God did in your situation, and your story is going to uplift and strengthen the people who hear it.

God is going to show up in your circumstances. Keep trusting and believing. Keep going.

Don't ever write people off and dismiss them as a hopeless cause. Their story isn't over yet. Maybe you're the one who is meant to enter at that pivotal point, and change the whole course of someone's life. All of our lives can get messed up and twisted, but miracles happen. Things can suddenly turn around in surprising ways. Maybe you're the one who God will use to save the day.

When your whole world is breaking apart, it might just be your breakthrough that you're witnessing. Maybe the shell surrounding you is what's been cracked and broken.

Let the light shine in.

Feathers out.

Wings outstretched.

Fly.

Kindness shown is kindness grown.

Those kindness seeds will spread.

The Wind is blowing...
where are they going?

The future's flowerbed.

We've all heard about the art of war, but what about the war of art? Art can defend and champion what is beautiful, what is true, what is pure, what is genuine, what is sincere, what is authentic, and what promotes love, peace and unity. Artists can defend and create a world that is closer to the heart through the beautiful expressions of our deepest thoughts and highest concepts.
Beauty and truth really are one.
Art can bring it all together.

You may think that other people have power over you, but you are the one who has power inside. It doesn't come from your possessions.
It doesn't come from people's perceptions. It's a God-given power, and it's part of you. Your time, your place, your purpose...is now.

You have the power.

If you vow to die hating someone, you will.

It's poison. Every moment of your life will be a death. Let it go. Release that person and yourself. Forgive and be free.

Live.

You can't drive your car by only looking in the rear view mirror. You have to see where you've been, but where you're going is so much more important. Look through your windshield.

Put your focus there.

Your future is in front of you.

Get yourself out there.
Put yourself on the line.

Go ahead and take the risk. Sure, you might suffer rejection, but you also might enjoy acceptance. If God has placed something on your heart to create, to do, to be, then by all means create it, do it, be it. Try and fail, but try again, with unshakeable persistence, with unwavering determination. Never give up. The next time might be the time that you succeed. Failure is just success in the making. Keep trying. Fail forward. Success is up ahead.

Hatred consumes the hater.

Don't give it a place in your head and heart.

Get it gone.

Choose to love.

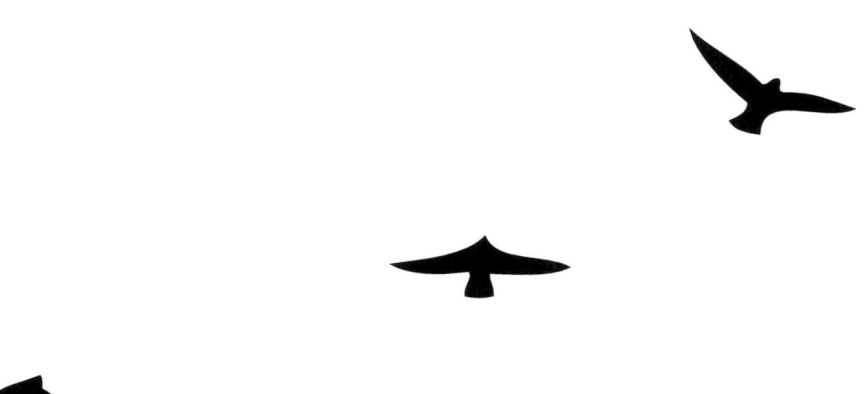

No false facades, no pretenses, no airs.
Be open. Be you. Your thoughts and cares.

Barriers gone. Wings waiting for flight.
Transparent as dawn. You let in the light.

A heart of compassion. A soul with a spark.
A candle uncovered. You light up the dark.

GROW

GIVE

CREATE

Change my heart.

Change my mind.

Change my life.

Give them a piece
of your mind?

or

Give them the peace
of your mind.

It's your choice.

Don't allow anyone to make you lose your mind.
Keep your composure. Stay sane. Stay calm.

You can give people a piece of your mind...or
you can give them the peace of your mind.

Peace or in pieces.

Choose peace.

Regardless of your particular situation,

the one necessary ingredient

in every recipe

is love.

Love makes everything better.

We all have our plans, but life
often unfolds in ways that defy our
preconceived notions. When should
we hold on and force things, and when
should we let go? A recurring idea in my
life is all about fishing. You won't catch
anything unless you're on the water, but
just being on the water is no guarantee. In
faith, you have to show up and be present
and believe that God will present the
opportunities. Be on the water and wait.
That's your part to play.
God will bring you what you need.

The more you fail, the more you succeed. That may sound strange, but it's a true principle, and a good recipe for success. Get out there and take chances. Leave your comfort zone and be vulnerable. Risk and have fun in the process. Let go and let the moments just happen. Don't assume you know everything. Keep asking. Be teachable. Be open to the unexpected and believe in miracles. Keep going and never ever give up. Success is a process, not a product.

Success is a process,

not a product.

The darkness is
overwhelming,
but there are many
cracks of light.

Just stretch your wings,
and that shell will be broken,
and you'll emerge for flight.

We tend to believe that when things are going well, that's an obvious sign that we're on the right track and doing what we're supposed to be doing. We assume that we'll be blessed if we're doing what is best, but that's not always the case. Sometimes when you resolve to stand up and do what you're being called to do, that's exactly when you'll be resisted and opposed the most. Maybe you're being fiercely attacked because you are directly over the target, and positioned where you need to be. Don't back down. Have faith. Be courageous. Keep going.

Your complete and total control of a situation does not always guarantee success, and in fact, might bring about the opposite. Let go of the outcome, and things may work out just as they should. Trust that. Believe it. "My way or the highway" is not always the answer. Letting go of your way might be the higher way. You think you know what's best, but maybe God knows better.

The answers start with questions.

The solution begins with a problem.

Puzzles come together in sections.

Dilemmas make you solve them.

Confusion is the beginning.

Being lost reveals the way.

You feel your world is spinning?

Darkness begins the day.

Live in unity,

with humility,

gentleness

and peace.

Past generational curses can become the
opportunity for future generational healing.

New beginnings can start
right now and right here.

Believe it.

When people discourage you,
frustrate you, slight you, offend you,
try your patience, annoy you, hurt
you or anger you, take a moment
and stop and remember that the
best response is not a reaction. Stop
the flow of where this is all heading.
Change the direction. Break the chain.
Give it to God and say to that person
(out loud or just in your head),
"How about I love you anyway,"
and then do that.

Keep loving.
Keep forgiving.
That's a beautiful thing.

Seeds are no ultimate good in piles and packets. Sanitary order does not bring them to life. They need to get dirty. They have to get messy. Sometimes the Wind scatters them and plants them where it will. The seeds aren't wasted when they fall into the mud. To the contrary, their purpose has just begun. The seeds didn't die going into the dirt.
They came alive.

Let it go. Trust the divine unfoldment of things.
Something beautiful
is going to grow.

Love endlessly
replenishes itself.

The more you give out, the
more love you
have left to give.

From God's mouth comes changed hearts.
Listen and be transformed,
and then transform the world.

Speak...
from your mouth to God's ears.
From your mouth comes a new reality.
This is the essence of prayer.

Encourage, uplift, speak blessings
over everyone, everywhere you go.
Do no harm.
Grow.
Give.
Create.
Feel love.
Think love.
Be love...

and act in loving ways.

Words create.
Everything around you was first an idea,
and then it was a spoken word.

Our concepts create things.
Concept precedes conception.
Conception precedes birth.
Our ideas give rise to 3-dimensional things.
Our thoughts are powerful.

Listen.
Think.
Speak.
Act.
The ripples will go out in amazing
and surprising ways.

You may have sold your soul to the devil, but guess what?

Jesus bought it back.

Don't walk away because
of your failures.

Failures are just stepping stones.
Keep walking.
Success is up ahead.

Whether you're the offended
or the offender,
the answer is the same:

FORGIVENESS.

Don't accept
authority as truth.

Accept truth as
authority.

I once had this dream. In my dream, I opened a
note card and read these words
(I woke up right away and wrote them down):

"You have the ability to be more, do more, and build a supply of income."

True story. True dream. Believing it and
living it out one day at a time.

Don't wait for opportunities.
Make them.

You have the power to do
what's inside you to do.
Start walking in that direction,
and those opportunities will
come your way.
It's a faith walk.
Start walking.

I heard it said that what we are is God's gift to us, but what we become is our gift to God, our families, our communities, and our world. Our gifts are called "gifts" because we've been given them, but also because we're meant to give them away in love and service to something greater than ourselves. Your life is a seed. What it grows into is partially your choice. The possibilities are endless. So, grow, give and create. Make the world a more beautiful place with all that only you can uniquely contribute. You are a gift. The world needs what only you can give.

Going nowhere on this blue ball.
Up we go and down we fall.
A lifetime circling around and around.
We kiss the sky, then hit the ground.

First in line, push and shove.
It all means nothing without love.
Nothing here can make you whole.
Gain the world and lose your soul.

Life is nothing without this:
Compassion, love and tenderness.
Be forgiven and then forgive.
A child of God will always live.

Borrowed money is not your salvation. When you bankroll your life, you're really just rolling a stone over a tomb of indebtedness. Don't do that. Trust God instead. Ask, seek, and knock. God gives freely without interest. His only interest is in you, in your liberation and freedom (and from so much more than mere financial things). Trust him for your daily provisions. Walk in faith and watch him show up on your behalf. Fix your eyes on Jesus, and God will fix your life. He gives freely. Mercy, forgiveness and renewal are waiting for you now. His hands are open. Just reach up and ask.

Write the wrongs and right the wrongs.

Expression can be the first step toward healing and making things right.

Quit quitting.

Quitting is something you need to quit.

Keep showing up and God will, too.
Stubbornness is not necessarily a
bad thing. Set your stubbornness on
refusing to give up until God shows up,
and watch what happens.

You can dissect, criticize and condemn things to death, and death will be the energy that you're generating. How about just loving people anyway, regardless of their flaws and shortcomings? How about speaking life over people instead of death?

I've heard that fear and faith have something in common: They both believe in something that hasn't happened yet. Hope is the confident expectation of God's goodness. Have faith. Let go of your fear.

The past you is gone.
Live like the new you:

In love, joy, peace, patience, kindness, goodness, faithfulness, gentleness and self-control. Begin to see every problem, obstacle and dilemma as an opportunity for God to upgrade your thinking and experience. All things work for good (even the bad things). Act and live like you believe it. Easier said than done, but don't give up. Keep going.

Imagination forms a map
that guides you to your goals.

Prayer is the path
that leads you there.

Flight occurs when the pressure from below is greater than the pressure from above.

What's pressing down on you?
What's keeping you down?
Quit focusing on your obstacles.
Instead, focus on your goals.

Surround yourself with those who will lift you up and be the wind under your wings. Press in and press on. Keep going. Those who are for you are greater than those who are against you. God wants you to soar. You'll be flying soon.

If you're running from your past, you can't really run into your future. They are two completely different trajectories. Lighten your load. Leave those past burdens behind you. They will only drag you down. You are forgiven and restored. Believe it and live it. New horizons await.

The best is yet to come.

Work, buy, consume and die?

That's not really living. It's a major step down from all we were created for. What are you doing with your gifts and talents? God gave them to you for a reason. Maybe your gifts are called "gifts" because you were meant to give them away in love and in service. Listen to your calling and go where it leads. It's a path to life.

Grow. Give. Create. Live.

Thoughts are things that make realities happen. They are the seeds that grow into the forests of our experience. If you don't like where you are, then start thinking different thoughts. Thoughts of love and positivity create more of the same. Negativity and hate are destructive. Don't allow them that precious place in the fertile soil of your head and heart. We can change our direction at any time. Turn around. Think differently. Do differently. Be forgiven and forgive others. Put negativity and hate behind you. Start afresh. God loves you. Believe it and live it. Love and be loved.

If you don't like what's being displayed on the screen of your life, then change the channel. Tune into something better. Fill your heart and mind with peace, light and love, and watch all the unrest, darkness and hate disappear. Change the setting. Focus on the good. Speak life and surround yourself with nurturing, life-giving things and people. Change your thoughts and your life will change. Your life is the overflow of everything you've allowed to enter your eyes, ears, mind and heart. Turn away from the things that have been destroying you. Walk into health and wholeness.

Your trials and tests become your testimony, and your mess becomes your message. The storm you're in right now will become that amazing story you're going to one day shout about. All things work for good. Believe it. Something wonderful is on the way.

Keep going.

All things work for good. We can take advantage
of every negative situation. No weapon
formed against you will prosper. That vertical
perspective will transform each negative into
a positive. Experiencing something negative?
Continue to look up. Be unshakeable. God will
transform that negative into something positive.
Just you wait and see. A wonderful intersection
is up ahead. Believe it. Keep going.
Your negative is about to become a positive.
We are more than conquerors in Christ.

The first four letters of 'painting' are 'pain'. That says it all. If you've ever done house painting, you may agree. Creating beauty might be painful, but the end product justifies the process. Creating art is turning our pain into something beautiful. Many artists are people who have turned their sorrows into something joyful, their struggles into something triumphant, and their dark valley experiences into something full of light and transcendence. Art brings a little bit of a heavenly perspective to our earthly experience. On Earth as it is in Heaven. Maybe that's why we create art?

On
ᴇARTʜ
as it is in
Heaven

When you're reviled, don't revile back. Don't react and return evil for evil. God is the one who will right every wrong. Do good to everyone, even your enemies (especially your enemies). Be silent. God's intervention on your behalf will be loud and clear.

Prayers up. Keep going. Your breakthrough is just up ahead. Believe it and live it, and soon you'll find it's already here. Your tongue is a rudder that will steer the ship of your life to its destination. Keep speaking life, encouragement and peace over everyone, everywhere, in every situation. Let light and love always be on your lips, and your words will be a map to the most amazing of places.

The miracle you need may already be in the house. We often have the answers to one another's prayers. In our prayers for someone else, we might even find that God will use us to be the fulfillment of that prayer. That was true of Forrest Gump's prayer for Jenny. He prayed that God would make her a bird so she could fly far, far away from all of her troubles, and it was Forrest who became the very wind under Jenny's wings that allowed her to transcend. He never ever gave up on her. His love and care for Jenny was unwavering and unfailing. He was the answer to her prayer.

The first four letters of 'painting' are 'pain'. Sometimes all we see is the pain, but press in and press on. The beauty of what God is in the process of painting with your life will be revealed soon enough, and the beauty of that painting will be well worth it. God may not be causing your pain, but he's going to use all of it for some ultimate good. Don't give up. Something beautiful is just up ahead. Your life is a work of art in the making. Keep going.

People get healed
when they get real.

Transparency lets in
the Light.

The place you're in is a place of preparation. You might want to escape the pain you're presently experiencing, but don't. You're where you are for a reason. God is doing something in the midst of what's happening at this moment. Keep going. Better days are ahead.

You may suffer great losses, but in that, you will find great gain. The impurities of your life will be burned up, but you will be refined and made better through it all.

Keep going.
Better days are ahead.

You can choose poisonous perceptions or life-giving visions. It's your choice. Focus on the good.

Experience what is best.

You may think your life is being destroyed, but you've got it wrong. God is building an amazing testimony in you. All you feel right now may be trauma and tragedy, but comfort (and even laughter) are right around the bend. Give it time. God is speaking life over you, and living is what you're going to do. Keep going. Better days are ahead.

Demolition sometimes precedes construction. What might appear to be destruction in your life, may actually be the clearing of the land for something better to be built.
Trust, wait and see.

God is building something wonderful.

When you feel like giving up,
maybe you should do exactly that:
Give it up to God, and watch the situation
change. It could be your unyielding control
of a particular situation that has caused it
to get out of control. Keep asking, seeking,
and knocking, but quit forcing. Maybe
you've been standing in the middle of the
flow, and it's been your presence that has
been blocking the solution.

Step aside.
Give it over to God.
Trust, believe and have faith.
Allow the answers to flow.

Fear retreats inward, but faith greets the day with confident expectation. Fear is paralyzing, but faith is liberating. Fear will lock you up in a dark and lonely place, but faith opens doors to fresh opportunities. It removes walls to reveal new horizons, and it replaces ceilings with the wide open sky. Fear shuts you down with obstacles, but miracles are the stepping stones of faith. Start walking. Go forward. Trust and believe. Amazing things are headed your way today. Have faith.

We can be so focused on what we don't have that we actually end up missing what we do have. Enjoy each day. Look for the beauty in every moment. Switch from grumbling to being grateful. Shift from negativity to thankfulness. It's really true that our attitude changes our experience, and our experience changes our reality. Quit focusing on the problem. Focusing on the problem is the problem. Thankfulness brings more things to be thankful for.

Embrace hatred.

Love works miracles.

What about hugging the hater?

Hate divides and destroys, but love
reconciles, heals and unites.
Keep putting it out there.
Love works miracles.

A vocation is not just a job. It's a calling. Before you can follow your calling, you first have to hear your calling. What direction are you being called to? What are you being called to do? Does that calling resonate with something deep inside of you? Do you know in your heart of hearts that it's right for you? It doesn't matter what others may say about the practicality or viability of the endeavor you're being called to. It may not be their calling, but that's not the issue. Are you being called to it?

Know your place.

Be confident.

Stand firm.

Hear that voice and walk toward it. You're headed toward your destiny.

Are economic realities like a gravitational force that is keeping you grounded? Are you stuck doing something to make a living that is killing you? Can you rise above the economic gravity and soar? I think a person's calling and passion are mixed together. As far as gravity goes, the history of human flight shows people looking foolish and awkward in their early attempts at flying, but in just over 100 years or so, we've gone from balloons to space travel. I think if you're being called to do something, take the leap of faith and start flapping your wings.

You'll never go wrong doing what is right.

Do you sing because you're happy,
or are you happy because you sing?

Declare it and make it so. Say it and sing
it out first, and soon you'll find that you
actually begin feeling it. Prime the pump
with praise, and your spirits will be lifted
in the process. A smile makes others smile.
Laughter brings more laughter. A friendly
person attracts friends. Love and be loved.
Gladness makes the heart glad.
Choose it even though you don't feel it,
and soon you'll be feeling just fine.

Sometimes we want an outward change, but what we really need is an inward change in our hearts and minds. So often, it's not where we are that matters as much as where our hearts are. A change in my latitude may not affect my psychological/emotional altitude at all. Will getting some promotion actually change my emotions? Temporarily, maybe, but in the long run, I end up being the same person in different circumstances. Attitude truly is everything. To be content in every situation is to be unshakeable. To be happy regardless of my circumstances would make me unbreakable. Is that possible? Is that an unreachable ideal? Perhaps, but I do believe that a change of heart will change your entire life.

We tend to believe that we create things with our hands only, but that is not the case. We also create things with our mouths. That may sound strange to say, but it's true. Our words not only communicate ideas, they also bring those ideas into reality. Words are like the dominoes in our hearts and heads that leave our lips and cause whole chain reactions to occur in the world around us. Words set things into motion. A single word can start a war or bring peace. Have someone's words ever hurt you deeply? Have someone's words ever given you happiness, courage or hope? Words are powerful. They can heal or destroy. Words convey ideas that are the triggers for change in the world around us. Words can be seeds to grow things, or they can be weapons.

Speak life. Don't speak death.

Lift people up with your words.

Encourage them. Speak blessings, not curses.

Life and death really are in the power of the tongue.

Who wants commotion in their lives? We'd all probably much rather have peace, but maybe that unwanted commotion is the very thing that's going to move us in the direction we're destined for. We may see it as chaos and commotion, but maybe it's the locomotion needed for our journey. Look at the commotion in your life differently. Where is God sending you? New horizons are just up ahead. New opportunities await.

Locomotion...full steam ahead.

Things will remain
uncertain as long as
you remain uncertain.

You receive it by seizing it.

Have faith and act on it.

Life's a faith-walk. Both the "faith" part and the "walking" part are important. Continue to walk on in faith, and God will give you the next stretch of road. New horizons unfold before us as we continue on our journey.

Have faith.

Keep going.

Wonderful things are up ahead.

Believe it.

Every day is a new day and a new beginning. Don't carry past limitations into your future. Keep going. New possibilities and opportunities await you today.

There's no shame in your past failures. Trust the process. Those failures were just the footsteps leading you to future victories. Those mistakes were just the stepping stones on the way to your destiny.

Believe it. Receive it. Wonderful things are on the way. Keep going. Love, forgiveness and new beginnings are yours today.

All the waves on the water...
all on one sea.
All the leaves on the branches...
all on one tree.
You and I fit together...
in one harmony.
You and I fit together...
in one family.

The power of perseverance saves the day (but that day may not be right away). It may not be immediate, but perseverance will get you through to that place of victory. Keep pressing in. Keep pressing on. Things will look different on the other side. You'll be there soon enough. Keep going.

Keep showing up regardless of how you feel.
Surrender your preconceived ideas and
know that your failure is not the end...
it's only the beginning.

Better days are ahead. Keep going.

Show up even when it's hard.
Don't lose your peace. God is crafting a bigger
backstory than you could even imagine.
God will put you where you are meant to be.

If you ever get to a place where you
think you've failed beyond repair,
you need to know that is a lie.

Focus on the good, and the good will come into focus in your life. We become what we focus on. What we focus on transforms us. We become what we think about. Focus on the good, the positive, the uplifting, the true, the pure, the holy, on what is kind, on what is compassionate, on what is merciful, on what is forgiving, and on what is life-giving.

Focus on the good.

The thoughts we allow in our heads are the film we project on the screen of our lives.

Your life is your movie screen. Change your thoughts and change your whole life.

Your thoughts are the film.
Your mind's the projector.
Your heart's the marquee.
You're the ticket selector...
of the show that waits to be seen.
Your life's your own movie screen.

Open the curtains. Step outside.
Take a long walk. Go for a ride.
Breathe the fresh air.
Wonders wait to be seen.
Your life's your own movie screen.

Being at the right place at the right time comes from having the right mindset and heart-set. Getting our hearts right and our minds right...that will overflow into all of our actions, our interactions, and our circumstances, and it will put us on the path of being in the right place at the right time continually.

Right heart, right mind, right place, right time.

N.E.W.S =
North, East, West and South

Don't just hear the
news of the day.

Make good news, and spread
good news everywhere you go.

If we go in that direction,
we can change the direction
of the world.

I've heard that the branch pattern is everywhere in nature because a branch pattern is the natural flow of energy. You can see the branch pattern everywhere in nature: in lightning, in rivers, in cracks, and in the branches of trees (and in family trees, too). I heard that the Hebrew word for 'son' means 'bough' (as in the bough of a tree), and the Hebrew word for 'daughter' means 'branch'. I love that! Sons and daughters are the boughs and branches on a family tree.

Without light, we're in the darkness.

Without warmth, we're in the cold.

Without love, we're lost on islands...

where no bridge or boat can go.

But there's a ship that's sailing...

across the lonely sea...

a bridge of love we're building...

connecting you and me.

Beauty…
it's internal and eternal…
and not just external and temporal.

Beauty truly is as beauty does.
Our beautiful actions, beautiful thoughts,
and beautiful emotions…they all overflow
into the world around us, and make that
world a more beautiful place for everyone.
That's a beautiful ideal.

Let's make it a beautiful reality.

Be YOUnique.

God gave you something totally unique.
Own it. You are more than enough. Don't
envy anyone else. Don't be jealous.
Look inside of yourself.
God deposited a treasure within you,
a treasure to enjoy and to share.
The world needs what only you can give.

Be you. Be YOUnique.

The sky is not the limit.
Our thoughts are.

Our limits are what we think they are
(for better or worse). The sky is not the limit.
Our thoughts are.

The joy is in the journey.

The joy is in the journey. It's easy to have our eyes so set on some preconceived destination that we miss the joy of living.
Be present in the present.
It's a gift. Unwrap it as you go.

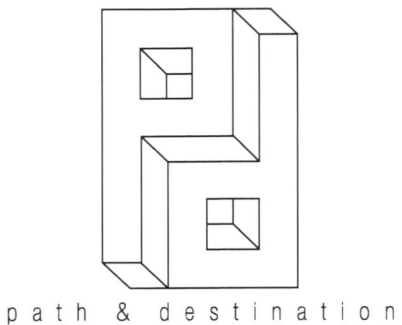

path & destination

The ends don't justify the means. What you are presently doing always sets the pattern for where you are going. The path is the destination. What you are doing (right here and right now) is exactly how you're going to get where you're headed.

Enjoy the journey.

The path is the destination.

On the road of life,
measure your journey in

smiles
(not in miles).

The joy is in the journey.

A new life isn't worlds away. It's only words away.

Speak life.

I love the analogy that the tongue is like a rudder of a ship. It might be small, but it's very powerful. Our words steer us toward our destiny (for better or worse). Be careful about the words you speak over yourself and others. You can build up or destroy with just words. Speak blessings, and speak life over yourself.

A new life is only words away.

Thoughts become words,
and words become actions,
and actions become reality.
Everything around us
was once just an idea in
somebody's head. Someone
thought it and spoke it (or
wrote it), and then created it.
What we think gets mirrored
in the world around us.
What we say gets echoed.
What we do comes back to us.

Thoughts matter. Thoughts become matter. Ideas take shape. Thoughts become form. Your thought life becomes your real life. Be careful about what you let into your head and heart. Ultimately, what you allow into your mind, you allow into your life. Thoughts matter because thoughts become matter.

Make wonderful things materialize.

Think beautiful thoughts.

Our memories see the past.
Our dreams see the future.

Think good thoughts.
Envision life.
Speak life.

Thoughts become words.
Words become actions.
Thoughts, words and actions become reality.

Words are boomerangs.

Speak blessings.

Our thoughts can make us healthy or sick. They can be like seeds growing beautiful things in our lives, or like a disease that negatively impacts our minds and bodies. Our thoughts are important. They become our words, and then they become our actions. Think beautiful things.
Speak them. Live them.
Pass them on.

Unity, not uniformity.
Diversity, not division.

Be yourself for the betterment of all.

Your uniqueness is for a greater purpose.
Own it and give it away.

The world needs what only you can give.

What is love?

In love, you lose yourself, but you also find yourself. You become part of something greater than yourself, and in that context, you are fulfilled. You die to yourself (in a way), but you also come alive. They say we "fall" in love, but it's in love that we rise...rising to something higher, while falling into something deeper, and transcending into something more beautiful. Love is hard to define exactly, but it defines us. What is the meaning of life? Maybe, it's love.

Maybe the meaning of life is found...
in the meaning of love.

You're not competing
with one another.

You're completing
one another.

That's love.

Be authentic.
Rise and shine.

The most powerful thing you can be is you.

Be authentic. Rise and shine.

FORGIVE

We've all done things and we've all
had things done to us, and the answer to
all that mess is this: forgiveness.

Give it. Receive it.
Pass it on. Today's a new day.

Forgive.

ACTIVATION

Don't wait for someone else to affirm you.
If you're wanting activation, you need to just
act and the "ivation" part will follow. Your
movement will start a whole new momentum.
Step into your calling today.
What are you waiting for?

Act and you will find your activation.

The law of gravity is overcome by the law of lift.

Whatever is dragging you down, it will be nullified by your motion, speed and direction.

Keep going. Don't give up.

You'll be flying soon.

Have faith.

Live that faith out.

Put energy behind that faith.

Work toward seeing that faith come to fruition.

there

You're here, but you're already there.

Live like the person you're becoming.
What you need, you already have. Speak life.
Live it in the here and now.

The same is true for everyone:
Here for a moment and then we're gone.

This life is like a single breath:
A quick sunrise and then sunset.

God, I give my life to you.
May I do all you want me to.

Breathe in me all your ways.
Be with me all my days.

The same is true for everyone:
Here for a moment and then we're gone.

This life is like a single breath:
A quick sunrise and then sunset.

Be transparent.

Let the Light in.

Thoughts and words
materialize.

Think and speak life,
love and hope.

Water and Fire...
The Potter's clay needs both.

The Water of Life allows us to be shaped.
The Fire of our circumstances solidifies our form.

Don't freak out about your circumstances.
Relax. Trust.
All things really do work for the good.
Something beautiful is being created
on the Potter's wheel of your life.

Believe it.

Keep showing up...
even when you're down.

Keep showing up, even when you're down.
Something may come your way today
that will change everything.
Don't be stuck reflecting on the past.
That thing that had you down is behind you.
Don't stay there.
Today's a new day with new possibilities.
Keep going.

You're not in a battle because you're doing something wrong. The battle is meant to shape you, define you and refine you. You are going to be totally transformed on the other side of this.

You're being transformed right now.

Be strong.

Keep going.

Life is all about
ME becoming WE.

If you take ME and turn it upside down,
you get WE.

I love that:
ME becoming WE...

like in a marriage, a family, a friendship

or a community.

ME becoming WE is a beautiful thing.

It's what life is all about.

OPPORTUNITYISNOWHERE

Opportunity is nowhere?
or
Opportunity is now here?

Maybe your problem is a solution in the making.
Every problem is a door. Go through it.
Your solution is on the other side.

Have faith that what you need will show up exactly when you need it. Faith is a bridge that materializes one step at a time. Start walking and the bridge you need will form beneath your feet. Where are you being called to go?

Listen and go in that direction.

Step out in faith.

Attitude is where it is at.

It really is all in your mindset. Be positive. Be hopeful. Be helpful. Believe. Your thoughts are the seeds of everything you plant in your life, and everything you grow. The things you want to blossom in your experience, those things are first given form in your heart and head. All that you want to come to fruition, all of that begins with your thoughts. Attitude is everything.

Life is a river,
and nothing you want is upstream.

Go with the flow into your future.
Go with the current...not against it. God
is taking you somewhere. A wonderful
destination awaits. Have faith and enjoy
the journey on the river of life. An ocean
is up ahead with wide-open horizons
and beautiful vistas.

Nothing you want is upstream.
Go with the flow.

When people are attacking you for
being who you are, just continue
to be who you are.
Who else would you be?

Your best contribution to other
people is for you to be you.
You be you and I'll be me.

Cooperation is not codependence.

Cooperation is good.
Codependence and coercion are not.

Your birdcage door is open.
You have wings to fly.

Sometimes we don't understand why we're waiting for certain things to come about. The best things take time. You may not be able to see and understand what God is doing in your life right now. The waiting can be hard, but guaranteed, it will be worth the wait. Keep believing. Keep hoping. Keep going. Something wonderful is on the way. Relax, trust, believe. You are not diminished in the waiting. In fact God is enlarging you while you wait (just like a pregnant woman). Something beautiful is growing while you're waiting. Be patient. Give it time. Something wonderful will be birthed soon enough, and all in God's perfect timing.

Tests are not meant to fail you. They are meant to fulfill you. They are not meant to shame you about what you don't know. Instead, they are meant to give you an opportunity to bring what you do know to the surface, and bring what you've learned into practice. The whole process is supposed to build you up, not tear you down. Leave your "life test" anxiety behind, and have fun in the process of learning and practice. You've got this. Let your awesomeness shine.

The meaning of life
is found in the
meaning of love.

Control the "rudder" of your boat (which is your tongue), and you will control the direction of your life. Your words steer your life. Speak encouragements, speak love, speak peace, speak blessings. Your words chart your course. Beautiful horizons are up ahead.
Think it. Believe it. Say it.

Keep going.

Maybe your distressing setback is actually a divine setup...for a bit of good fortune that you cannot see and appreciate just yet.
All things work for good. Trust that there's a greater wisdom at work in this situation. Believe it.
Something better is on the way.

Be confident of that.

Keep going.

Frozen rivers flow again,

and joy replaces pain.

From prison snows, green shoots rise

toward prismed skies of rain.

In winter, I wait
for the freeze to end,
for leaves to appear,
for summer again.

I wait for you.

Your starlight kisses.
Your sunset eyes.
My darkness misses
your heart's sunrise.

I wait for you.

Speak the solution.

Don't speak your circumstances.

Don't speak the wreckage of what went wrong.

Speak the Word.

You are not "done for"...
you are not "finished" (in the negative sense).
The truth is just the opposite. God sees you
perfected. God sees you finished. What you will
be in the end is wonderful, and that is actually
what you already are right now. Place your
sights on that. Place your hope in that. Relax and
rest, and trust in that truth.
Like a flowerbud that is opening, you are
becoming what you already are. Rest in the
unfoldment of that beauty. Grow into what you
were made to be. Keep going.
Blossom and bloom.

We speak from the overflow of what's inside of us. Fill yourself up with positive things, with beautiful things, with encouraging things, uplifting things, constructive things, creative things, things of love, joy and peace. Be filled with those things, and those things will overflow from your lips, into your life, and into the lives of the people around you. Is someone speaking negative words toward you? Don't receive it, and don't return evil for evil. Bless them. Maybe someone filled them up with negativity somewhere along the way. Stop the negative domino chain right there and then.
Love that person. Your positive words and actions might change their whole day...
and maybe their whole life.
We speak from the overflow
of what's inside of us.
Be filled up with what is best,
and let it flow into your world.

Things are ideas before they take form. Actions are thoughts before they are movements. A house starts with a blueprint. The same is true with our daily lives. We think and say things into being. Concepts get conceived, and those plans get produced. Those matters we're thinking about in our heads really do materialize. "As a man thinks in his heart, so is he." We determine the outcomes of situations by our actions, but also, first and foremost, by our thoughts and then by our words. Those thoughts and words become actions. They materialize. Ideas activate the world around us, but that activation first starts with us. What's in your heart? What's on your mind? Your thoughts and words are powerful. Think higher thoughts. Speak them into being. Act on them. Bring love, peace, harmony and healing into existence. Change your words and change the world.
"As a man thinks in his heart, so is he."

Your head is the doorway to what you become.
All those things we allow
inside of us, they transform us:

The food we eat.
The things we drink.
The music we listen to.
The media we consume.
All the things we choose to read.
The images we open our eyes and hearts to.

Your head really is the doorway
to what you become.

You decide what you let inside.

Negative words are like a virus.
They only spread more negativity, but positive
words are like seeds. They multiply, they grow,
they blossom and bloom. Your good words will
bring harvest after harvest of good things.

Be kind. Be encouraging. Be loving.

Speak words that grow, give, and create.
Your world will be what your words say it is.

Speak life.

Your perceived problem may actually be the
seed of a solution that you could never imagine
or make happen on your own. Keep believing.
Keep going. Keep looking for all the good that
God has on the way for you.
Stop talking about the problem.
Speak the solution instead.
Your turnaround is here.

The sound of the waves
as they crash on the shore.

The gulls on the wind
as they hover and soar.

We walk hand in hand
and we need nothing more.

Sunset, sublime,
starry-still to the core.

Your well may have dried up so that you would move forward to a river. Your puddle may have evaporated because there was an ocean just waiting for you to become desperate enough to find it. You are not in a desert. Walk over the sand in front of you, and you will see that endless waters are waiting for you.
There are oceans of opportunity
just over the dunes.

We definitely create things with our thoughts, that become our words, that become our actions. Every product we see around us was once just a thought inside someone's head (for better or worse). It's so important to think and speak things that grow, give and create. Life and death really are in the power of the tongue. It's the rudder that steers the boat of our lives toward the horizons of our choosing.

Think it.
Say it.
Do it.
Go.

There's a balance between becoming and being content where you are right now. The joy is in the journey. Go forward toward your goals, but enjoy everything along the way.
Be thankful for your today...
as you head into your tomorrow.

A negative mindset can suck the life right out of you (and everyone around you). Our thoughts become our words, and our words become our actions, and our actions become our reality. It's a whole domino chain, and it starts with our mindset. Believe, and think, and hope for the best. Start being thankful, and you'll begin to see more things to be thankful for. A negative word from someone can too easily ruin your day, but don't let it. Turn it around and choose to speak blessings over yourself and others. Life and death really are in the power of the tongue. Speak life. Practice it. Live it.

Your frame of mind is determined by what you choose to place in your mind's frame. What you focus on comes into focus in your life, and will become the content and color of your thoughts, emotions, circumstances and relationships.

Turn your problem around and you might find your solution right there in the midst of it. Maybe that problem only came about so a beautiful solution could be discovered. Maybe your dilemma is actually a doorway. What you perceived to be a barrier might actually be a blessing in disguise. Don't give up. Keep going. The answers to your prayers might be right here, and you've been overlooking them.

The Creator of the universe created you to be creative, too. Think about that. What were you made to create with your unique life, time and talents? We are all parts of a diverse grand design. It's not a static and stagnant creation. It's living, breathing, unfolding, growing and blossoming, and you are a part of it. You were created to bring amazing and beautiful things into fruition. Creativity flows inside of you. It's part of your DNA. It's your birthright. Use your unique voice, perspective, ideas and vision to transform the world around you. Your hands carry a one of a kind fingerprint, and what you do with those hands will be equally as unique.

on
eARTh
as it is
in
Heaven

(this is why we create art)

Look for the beauty in creation, and you'll find
it. If you find it, then share it with others. Maybe
life is a scavenger hunt for treasure, to find all
the beauty that's hidden in creation. Finding
that beauty, uncovering it, and sharing it with
others...that is what makes life true living.
The beauty in creation brings us to life.
That beauty gives us wings to fly.

Thanks to my friends and family for a lifetime of unfailing love. Nests, trees, horizons and skies have deeper meaning because of you.

Also, to Heartprint Writer's Group and the Writing Room, thanks for your friendship, constant encouragement and continual inspiration. You have kept me dreaming, writing, moving forward... and trying out my wings.

Thanks to everyone at Olive Tree Connections for the love, prayers, prophetic words and eternal perspectives. I am a better person because of you. There is healing in His wings.

Selah Press, you put the feather pen in my hands, opened the birdcage, and then opened the window on this project. Thanks for all your help.

You can check out my music at:

https://www.reverbnation.com/pauldengler

and

https://www.collisionpointpublishing.com/pauldengler

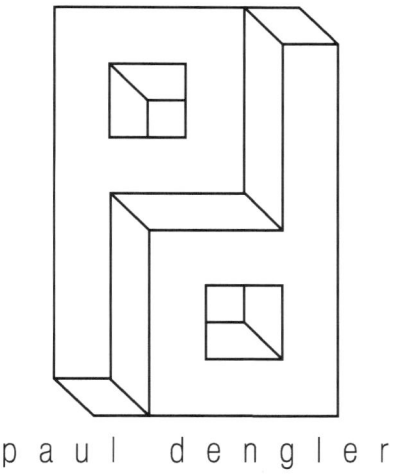

p a u l   d e n g l e r

pauldengler.com

Made in the USA
Columbia, SC
31 August 2020